Norman Jacobs & Kerry O'Quinn present

space art

Compiled and written by Ron Miller
Art Director: Robert P. Ericksen
Designer: Phyllis Cayton

Editors: Jon-Michael Reed, Robin Snelson
Art Staff: Laura O'Brien, Susan Stevens
Asst. Publisher: Ira Friedman

About The Wrap-around Cover:
Saturn, as seen from its moon, Titan, is almost the trademark of Chesley Bonestell. At age ninety, Bonestell is the quintessential astronomical artist. For the cover of SPACE ART, Bonestell visited Titan once again to paint this famous scene, based on the latest scientific findings. He describes the painting: "Constantly and totally cloud-covered, Saturn, seen from its largest satellite, Titan (3,000 miles in diameter), subtends an angle of approximately six degrees from a distance of 759,000 miles. Seen here through a normal visual angle (approximately forty degrees), it covers one-seventh of the sky. Titan is known to be reddish and to hold a thin atmosphere, and is probably covered with patches of frozen atmosphere, or "snow," due to its extreme cold."

STARLOG PRESS
O'Quinn Studios, Inc.
Norman Jacobs/Kerry O'Quinn
475 Park Avenue South
New York, NY 10016

Entire contents of Space Art is copyrighted © 1978 by O'Quinn Studios, Inc. Reprinting or reproduction in part or in whole, without written permission of the publishers, is strictly forbidden. All rights reserved. First printing, 1978. Second printing, 1979.

Preface

Neil Armstrong was *not* the first person to set foot on the Moon. Hundreds of thousands of men, women, and children had already been there and were watching that historic television broadcast in 1969 just to see if NASA's discoveries would live up to the visions we had already seen.

Earlier visions had been supplied, not by scientists, but by artists — by Chesley Bonestell, Fred Freeman, and Rolf Klep, among others. These painters and illustrators had engaged in an important human process called extrapolation.

Strictly defined, extrapolation means to infer an *unknown* from something that *is* known. In the visual arts, the process of inferring leads to more than just guesses and reasoned conclusions — it leads to realistic pictures. Viewers can do more than appreciate the abstract speculation of scientists and astronomers, we can *see* them in concrete reality.

Space artists make it possible for us to walk on the Moon.

Good extrapolation requires a keen mind — one that can understand the frontiers of knowledge in the various sciences involved, and can fill in the gaps with reasoned assumptions that are not out of line with the known facts.

And, of course, the professional space artist must also be a master of rendering techniques and possess a vivid sense of imagination, of wonder, and of the Romantic spirit.

If one saw a classified job ad that listed the necessary skills for a space artist position, most good artists would find that they need not bother to apply.

Space artists are special people, miles above the arbitrary splashers and dribblers who clutter Madison Avenue galleries, yet the artistic abilities of space artists have never received the serious attention and praise from critics that they deserve. And their cultural contributions — their inspiration to scientists and to the public — have likewise remained unrecognized.

It is toward correcting that error that this book is dedicated — the first ever devoted exclusively to space art.

Kerry O'Quinn / 1978

Contents

Artist Index 7
Introduction: In the Beginning 8
The Archaeology of Space Art 10
The Masters of Space Art
    Chesley Bonestell 20
    Bob McCall 30
    Ludek Pesek 38
    Lucien Rudaux 44
The Big Back Yard
    Mercury 50
    Venus 56
    Earth 58
    The Moon 62
    Mars 70
    Jupiter 80
    Uranus 88
    Neptune 90
    Pluto 92
Everybody's Favorite Planet: Saturn 94
Comets, Etc. 108
The Galaxy and Its Worlds 112
How We'll Get There: The Hardware Artists 122
The Universe and the Imagination 140
The NASA Fine Arts Program 148
The Great 1951 Space Program 164
About Some of the Artists 176
Where to See Space Art 182
Where to Buy Space Art 184
The Making of a Space Painting 186
Selected Bibliography 190
Acknowledgements 191
About the Author 192

Artist Index

Arlt, Paul...**163**

Bayard, Emile...11
Beard, Dan..12,**17**
Bensusen, Sally.....................................**88**, 176
Berkey, John.......................................122, 185
Bittinger, Charles.....................................17, **19**
Bolton, Scriven..........................15, **16**, 20, 44
Bonestell, Chesley........cover, 9, 10, 14, 15, 17, 20, **21-29**, 44, **58, 63, 66-67**, 76, **81, 85**, 99, **102**, 120, 122, **132, 137**, 164, **166-167, 169, 173**, 183, 185-186
Brown, Howard V.....................................**87**
Buinis, Lonny.......................................**103**
Butler, Howard Russell...........................15, **59**

Calle, Paul....................**156-157, 160, 162**, 183
Clark, John...**130**
Clement, Hal..................................**114-115**, 186
Coggins, Jack.................**67, 135, 138-139**, 176
Crane, Ray..**140**, 176
Cunningham, James...........................**145**, 176

Davis, Don...........**60, 74-75**, 102, **115**, 119, 122, 177
deNeuvill, A..11
DiFate, Vincent................................**136**, 177, 185
Dixon, Don........**56, 62, 64-65, 80, 92-93, 107**, 119, 177, 185
Dodd, Lamar......................................153

Egge, David....................................**57, 87**, 177
Emerson, Gilbert...................................17

Foss, Chris.......................................122
Freeman, Fred...**134**, 153, 164, **170, 174-175**, 177-179, **188-189**

Hardy, David.........**110-111, 112-113, 124-125**, 178, 185
Hardy, Paul.....................................12, **81**
Hartmann, William K............9, **68**, 178, 183, 185
Hervat, James..............**51, 77, 98, 107**, 178-179, 185
Hunter, Mel...................................**68, 141**

Jamieson, Mitchell..............................**161**
Jane, Fred T...12

Kent, Rockwell......................................17
Klep, Rolf...........................164, **168, 170-172**, 178
Krasyk, Francis J..................................**151**

Lehr, Paul....................................**142-143**, 179, 183
Leigh, W.R..**13**

Lothers, John..17

MacDonall, Angus..................................**10**
McCall, Bob...........................30, **31-37**, 183
Mead, Syd....................................**128**, 185
Meigs, John......................................**157**
Miller, Ron.......**72, 78-79, 86, 94, 99, 106, 116-117**, 185, 192
Miller, Tom..**89**, 179
Mion, Pierre....................122, **133, 139**, 179, 183
Moreaux, Abbe Theophile...........15, 44, **95**, 179
Morghen, Filippo...................................11
Mullins, Jay......................................**126**

Nasmyth, James.............................12, 44, **67**

Olson, John......................................**126**

Palmstrom, William................17, 19, **58, 129**
Paul, Frank R..................................15, **136**
Pesek, Ludek...........19, 38, **39-43, 52-53, 70-71, 73, 90-91, 96-97, 100-101, 104-106, 108**, 183, 185-186
Phillipoteaux, P.........................11, **15, 102**
Pitz, Henry C..................................**154-155**

Rauschenberg, Robert.................**149**, 153, 183
Rockwell, Norman...........................**158-159**, 179, 183
Rose, Sheila....................**54-55, 144**, 179, 183, 185
Rudaux, Lucien.....14-15, 19, 20, 44, **45-49, 57, 61, 66, 68, 76, 102**, 179

Schaller, Adolf......................**82-83**, 179, 183, 185
Schneeman, Charles................................17
Schoenherr, John............................**120**, 179
Schomburg, Alex.........................**103, 118**, 180
Smith, R.A.....................12, **61, 131, 135**, 180
Sokolov, Andrei.....................**127, 147**, 180, 185
Solovioff, Nicholas..............................**160**
Stevens, D. Owen.................................**121**

Watt-Geiger, Denise............................**123**, 181
Weymouth, George..............................**160**
Whelan, Mike....................................**144**, 181
Williams, Leroy..................................**132**
Willis, John.....................................**152**
Wimmer, Helmut............................**146**, 181
Wood, Stanley L..............................12, **18**
Wright, H. Seppings................................12
Wyeth, James...................................**150**

Note: Bold face page numbers indicate art reproductions.

7

In The Beginning

Unlike many space artists who have picked up astronomy on the way, I did it backwards, by becoming a professional astronomer (Ph.D. astronomy, M.S. geology, B.S. physics) who picked up painting on the way.

Like many space artists and scientists, I was influenced as a teenager in the 1950s by the Chesley Bonestell images appearing in magazines and in books like *The Conquest of Space*. I am convinced that visionaries such as Bonestell, by creating images of places where humanity could go before we had the technology to go there, played a subtle but major role in getting us off the Earth. They affected a generation of youngsters who later became the scientists and technicians that turned the dream into reality. Someone had to create the original image—the idea. Today's space artists play that role for the next century.

It is interesting that many scientists who may have started off as youngsters, impressed in this visual way, have evolved into scientists who have lost a sensory feel for their work. Schools and careers in science and technology today (but not always in the past or perhaps future) tend to train students away from visual dreams, because the greatest success in making workable machines and theories has come from the analytic approach of breaking systems down into mathematically analyzable parts. It has to be this way for us to build things. But that doesn't mean that our visual imaginations need to atrophy.

Painting forces us to synthesize everything we know from science, nature, and art to produce the scenes that our instruments measure. It is bad enough that the public has a hard time visualizing the extraordinary scenes that exist elsewhere in space. But even the scientists who discover these scenes apparently often don't visualize them.

I have had the experience of attending scientific meetings where new phenomena were announced and talking to the discoverer (who may have announced, for example, a luminous glow with a brightness measured in some obscure scientific units). I said, "What would that actually look like to the human eye if you could stand there and see it? Is it bright enough to be visible?" No answer. The question had never even occurred to my friend.

Perhaps it is a state of elevated scientific grace when the effects you measure are so detached from ordinary reality that you don't even know if they'd be detectable by the body—but, I don't think so. Space artists of the realist school have a role to play. They can make us aware of what we are discovering out there. And, space artists of the fantastic school make us aware of unimagined possibilities.

WILLIAM K. HARTMANN
Senior Scientist
Planetary Science Institute
Tucson, Arizona

Artist unknown, from The Book of Popular Science, *1924.*

The Archaeology of Space Art

Angus MacDonall, from Drowsy, *1914.*

Even the most realistic portrait artist, if he's creative, brings a vivid imagination to his studio, along with paints and brushes. The goal of the artist is to look at reality, to form a personal impression of it, and to develop the skills necessary to render the impression in objective terms. The artist is constantly weighing the photographic rendering of reality against the recreation he can construct through his own imagination. And the balance he selects between naturalism and imagination often becomes the artist's identifiable style.

The artist is normally allowed great latitude in his adherence to reality. If the flowers in his studio still-life are wilted, he is permitted to paint them as if they were freshly cut. Personal selectivity is a key element in good painting and gives art an emotional power that photography can never equal. Yet, there is one category of art in which departures from reality oppose the purpose of the art.

The purpose is to visualize a part of reality which is "unseeable," and the person who does this is the scientific artist.

The two sciences which the scientific artist pursues are paleontology (with its inability to see anything but petrified bones) and astronomy (with its numbing mathematics and interminable star fields which are incomprehensible to anyone but the scientists involved). Both sciences need to have their subject matter visualized in realistic, concrete terms—not just laboratory symbols and other mumbo-jumbo.

When the scientific artist creates an accurate vision of the unseen objects, he not only provides inspiration to those working in the field, but he forms a method of communication to the rest of the world: the non-scientific public. In the case of astronomical art, there is little question that the taxpayers of the world were rallied behind the space program largely due to popular illustrated magazine articles and books—like the *Collier's* and *Life* series of the '50s and the now-classic books by Chesley Bonestell, with text by Wernher von Braun, Willy Ley, and others.

The astronomical artists of the last few decades had as much to do with the success of the space effort as any technical advances. Just as early American artists showed the public views of the unconquered West and helped propel interest in exploration and expansion (as artists of vision and realistic imagination always point the way), so, too, astronomical artists have shown the public what the unseen planets, moons, comets, and distant reaches of the galaxy might look like when we are able to be there in person.

And, as a result, just as the field of astronomy has produced eminent scientists, it has also produced several great artists.

Before the time of Jules Verne, flights to the Moon were visually depicted with the aid of geese and demons. The moon environment contained a world of pumpkin-houses (Filippo Morghen, in a picture-book engraved in the late eighteenth century) or mountains of ruby (Richard Locke's *The Moon Hoax*, 1835). Even according to the limited astronomical knowledge of the time, there were no visions of what could or should be expected. Rather, the visions were simply allegorical outlets for the authors' and artists' social, religious, or occult beliefs.

The famous stories of travel to the Moon by Cyrano deBergerac and Edgar Allan Poe were solely vehicles for satire on contemporary society. Johann Kepler's *Somnium* (1634) demonstrated that this wasn't necessary. His *method* of getting to the Moon is supernatural. (Space-travel stories of every age employ means of travel that are best accepted by the intended audience. For example, Verne employed a giant cannon to launch his manned projectile, because the rocket was in such an early stage of development that none of his readers would have believed rockets to be realistic.) But Kepler's Moon is not supernatural.

"Night is fifteen or sixteen days long, and dreadful with uninterrupted shadow," Kepler wrote. His Moon is similar to our world except that mountains are much higher and more rugged, with deep valleys and fissures. Kepler was also aware of the Moon's extreme climate, the weightlessness and the airlessness of space, and was the first writer to propose lunar inhabitants with a biology to suit their environment. Had *Somnium* been illustrated, it might have provided us with the first true astronomical art.

The first space art appeared in 1865 with the illustrations by Emile Bayard and A. de Neuvill for Jules Verne's novel, *From the Earth to the Moon*. As mentioned, there had been imaginary views of other worlds, and even of space flight, before this. But until Verne's book appeared, these views all had been heavily colored by mysticism rather than science.

The illustrations accompanying *From the Earth to the Moon* and its sequel, *A Trip Around the Moon*, were the first artistic impressions of space ever created strictly according to scientific fact. This was no accident. Verne, a meticulous researcher of facts, was in the habit of overseeing the illustrations of his novels. His prime interest in creating his stories was to present a series of scientific or geographical facts which were sugar-coated with a good story. And he realized that the illustrations that went with his stories must conform to fact as well. For these books, Verne even had a lunar map specially drawn by Beer and Maedler, the leading selenographers of the day.

In 1877, Verne published *Off On a Comet*, with illustrations by P. Phillipoteaux of such scenes as Jupiter and its moons as seen from a passing asteroid and Saturn's rings as seen from the surface of that planet. In the novel itself, there is a passage evocative of the following century of space art:

"To any observer stationed on the planet, between the extremes of lat. 45 degrees on either side of the equator, these wonderful rings would present various strange phenomena. Sometimes they would appear as an illuminated arch, with the shadow of Saturn passing over it like the hour-hand over a dial; at other times they would be like a semi-aureole of light. Very often, too, for periods of several years, daily eclipses of the sun must occur through the interpositions of this triple ring.

"Truly, with the constant rising and setting of satellites, some with bright discs at their full, others like silver crescents, in quadrature, as well as by the encircling rings, the aspect of the heavens from the surface of Saturn must be as impressive as it is gorgeous."

In 1874, James Nasmyth and James Carpenter published their classic study of the Earth's satellite, *The Moon*. A large and lavishly illustrated volume, its numerous plates were reproductions of photographs of plaster models of portions of the lunar surface, seen both telescopically from Earth and as they would appear to an observer on the Moon. The models, and the one or two paintings in the book, were all created by James Nasmyth, one of the pioneers of lunar origin theory.

The year 1887 saw the beginning of the *Cassell's Family Magazine* serial, "Letters from the Planets," by W.S. Lach-Szyrma (completed in 1893). It is the story of a tour that visits the Sun, Mercury, Mars, and the moons of Jupiter. The series had illustrations by Paul Hardy, which reflect the astronomical facts and theories of the time. For example, it was thought that the Sun's heat was maintained by the impact of the millions of meteorites that must hourly fall into it. The serial, "Stories of Other Worlds," by George Griffith (later published in book form as *Honeymoon in Space*) appeared in 1900 and was profusely illustrated by Stanley L. Wood. Once again, planetary surfaces are shown in the light of contemporary science. However, a visit to the Moon is shown in two excellent illustrations of the hero and heroine in very realistic space suits, exploring a convincing lunar surface.

For a period of years at the end of the last century, artist and writer Fred T. Jane produced a series of illustrations for *Pall Mall* magazine, entitled "Guesses at Futurity." Some of these, such as "Gold Mining in the Mountains of the Moon," are remarkably similar to the moon colonies pictured sixty years later by British Interplanetary Society artist R.A. Smith.

A Journey in Other Worlds by John Jacob Astor was illustrated by Dan Beard (who founded the Boy Scouts) and published in 1894. The book begins with a tour of the world of 2000 AD (which proves that Astor was a brilliant and pre-

Above: *By H. Seppings Wright, from* Splendour of the Heavens, *1927.*
Right: *By W. R. Leigh, from* Cosmopolitan, *1905.*

> "Magic has paved the way for science."
> — Sir James Frazer
> The Golden Bough

scient engineer) and continues to a flight to Jupiter that contains descriptions of that world, which, although wrong by today's science, would do justice to Hal Clement or Arthur C. Clarke. The novel also contains a description of "Cassandra," the tenth, trans-Neptunian planet (Pluto's discovery was still over thirty years in the future), that is incredibly prophetic:

". . . the sun, though brighter, appears no larger than the Earth's evening or morning star. Cassandra has also three large moons; but these, when full, shine with a pale grey light. . . . The temperature at Cassandra's surface is but little above the cold of space, and no water exists in the liquid state, it being as much a solid as liquid or glass. There are rivers and lakes, but these consist of liquefied hydrogen and other gasses, the heavier liquid collected in deep places, and the lighter . . . floating upon it without mixing, as oil on water . . . were there mortal inhabitants on Cassandra, they might build their houses of blocks of oxygen or chlorine . . . and use ice that never melts, in place of glass. . . .

"Though Cassandra's atmosphere, such as it is, is mostly clear . . . the brightness of even the highest moon is less than an earthly twilight, and the stars never cease to shine. The dark base of the rocky cliffs, is washed by a frigid tide, but there is scarcely a sound, for the pebbles cannot be moved by the weightless waves. . . ."

During and immediately following the turn of the century, many popular books on astronomy were published and illustrated with space art. The most outstanding illustrator of such books, Lucien Rudaux, was also the first genuine astronomical artist. Rudaux (1874-1947) was both an artist and a professional astronomer. He wrote and illustrated a number of texts, such as the authoritative (and still in print) *Larousse Encyclopedia of Astronomy*. For his work, Rudaux received many awards, including the Legion of Honor, and more recently, a Martian crater was named after him (see Masters of Space Art chapter).

Although Chesley Bonestell was later to make the concept of a craggy moonscape the most popular image, the Moon, as Rudaux painted it in the 1920s and '30s, was a bland, rolling landscape, with rounded, sloping mountains. In fact, many of Rudaux's lunar scenes look uncannily like

Apollo photographs. Ironically, Rudaux wrote in 1926:

"It is astonishing...what phantastic representations have been drawn of the landscapes of this lunar world. Numerous astronomical treatises have represented them as embellished with mountains and peaks made of jagged sugar loafs, at the feet of which are heaped numerous small vatlike formations having the appearance of volcanic molehills."

The Illustrated London News of the 1920s was to space art what *Life* was later to become in the '50s. Rudaux was a frequent contributor, as was Scriven Bolton, who began the technique of constructing model landscapes set against painted backgrounds. His work can be found in many books, notably the lavishly illustrated, two-volume *Splendour of the Heavens* (1927). He was joined in this book by the Abbe Moreux, whose work dates from the late 1800s. Although Bolton and Moreux did excellent work, their many mistakes inspired a young artist, who had been executing architectural renderings for the *Illustrated London News,* to "indulge in space painting." The young artist was Chesley Bonestell (see Masters of Space Art chapter).

An American artist of this era, Howard Russell Butler, N.A. (1836-1934), produced many painterly space scenes. To render his canvases of solar eclipses, Butler would even travel on solar eclipse expeditions to witness the actual events. Many of his paintings are in the collections of the American Museum of Natural History and the Smithsonian Institution.

By P. Phillipoteaux, from Off on a Comet, *1877.*

Frank R. Paul (1884-1964) produced an unbelievable volume of work during his career—primarily for Hugo Gernsback's many publications, particularly *Science and Invention* and *Amazing.* He was trained as an engineer and architect, and his hardware (if nothing else) was drawn convincingly and authoritatively, although always with an odd flavor of art nouveau. His astronomical work was always a little more imaginative than anything else painted in the field at the time. Paul produced

Left: *By Scriven Bolton, from* Splendour of the Heavens, *1927.*
Top: *Artist unknown, from* A Study of the Sky, *1896.*
Above: *By Dan Beard, from* Journey in Other Worlds, *1894.*

some excellent work, such as the illustrations for *Science and Invention* which depict some of the strange visual effects of Saturn's rings.

For the November 1, 1937, issue of *Life* magazine, Rockwell Kent provided four stylish lithographs, illustrating as many possible ends for our Earth. Kent was one of this nation's most highly regarded artist-illustrators, still famous for his classic artwork for *Moby Dick,* Boccaccio's *Decameron,* and his own *N by E.* His lithographs for *Life* anticipate Bonestell's 1953 *End of the World.* Coincidentally, Chesley Bonestell once collaborated on an eighty-foot mural with Kent, in Maine, circa 1920.

For the April, 1939, issue of *Astounding,* Charles Schneeman created one of the finest of all pre-Bonestell astronomical paintings. During his long career he produced many superb astronomical cover paintings. The illustrations by Charles Bittinger for the July, 1939, *National Geographic* show how far ahead even the science-fiction pulps of the '30s were in the accurate depiction of astronomical concepts. Bittinger's paintings were among the very first astronomical art to appear in a nationally distributed popular magazine and were described as "combining a fine sense of color values and artistic composition with a painstaking effort to achieve scientific accuracy." But with one or two possible exceptions, they are rather crudely done and the science is only slightly better. Bittinger later did other space and scientific subjects for the *Geographic.* He covered a solar eclipse expedition, was official artist for Task Force One, and recorded the Task Force's first atomic bomb experiments in the Pacific in the late '40s.

National Geographic redeemed itself two decades later by way of the art that accompanied the article, "How Man-Made Satellites Can Affect Our Lives," in the December, 1957, issue. The art was by staff illustrators John Lothers, William Palmstrom, and Gilbert Emerson. These artists created some of the most beautiful paintings of satellites in

orbit yet published (at a time when only the Soviets had a satellite in space). Palmstrom had also, in another issue, painted the Earth as it would appear in space: probably the best and most accurate such painting done since Lucien Rudaux's similar attempts in the '30s. Of course, it was also the *Geographic* that first introduced Ludek Pesek to American audiences, in 1970.

Astronomical art blossomed after the 1950s. In the years immediately before and following the launch of Sputnik I (1957), the space art that appeared in magazines, such as *Collier's, This Week,* and *Coronet,* and in books, such as *The Conquest of Space* and Arthur C. Clarke's *Exploration of Space* (which was a 1951 Book-of-the-Month Club selection), helped convince the public that space exploration was far from a fantasy and that it was well within the reach of contemporary science and engineering. Beyond the question of hardware, realistic and accurate paintings of other worlds showed that the moons and planets were not as insubstantial as fuzzy astronomical photographs made them seem, but were genuine worlds in their own right.

There are more artists illustrating space subjects today than all those in the past combined. This is due partly to the increased interest in space travel and the broad range the subject allows the artistic imagination.

Modern space artists have both an easier and, at the same time, more difficult job than the space artists of a generation ago. More discoveries have been made about the nature of our neighboring planets in the last decade than in all the previous history of astronomy. Contemporary artists certainly have more factual material to draw upon, yet this abundance also limits them. We *know* what the surface of Mars looks like now—there is far less leeway for the artist's own imagination. The phrase "artist's impression" attached to a space painting no longer means an imaginary guess. □

Above: *The Earth, seen from the Moon's surface,* by Charles Bittinger, N.A. (copyright National Geographic Society).
Opposite: *By Stanley Wood, from* Honeymoon in Space, *1900.*

The Masters of Space Art

CHESLEY BONESTELL

When Chesley Bonestell was born, the Wright Brothers were only seventeen and twenty-one, and Robert Goddard, the inventor of the liquid-fueled rocket, was a mere six years of age. The hottest news in aviation was the flight of the first gasoline-powered balloon, and Jules Verne still had half his writing career ahead of him. H.G. Wells was not quite twenty-two and as yet unpublished. Ninety years later, Bonestell is still hard at work. His lifetime embraces the first manned airplane flight and the first Moon landings. He was not the first artist to work with astronomy, but the extraordinarily high level of quality and integrity in his work, as well as its wide-spread visibility, raised astronomical art to the level of a distinct artistic genre.

Bonestell's original training—and first love—was architecture. He began his career as an architectural renderer and designer, with several prominent San Francisco homes to his credit. In the 1920s, he worked for the *Illustrated London News,* doing renderings of famous buildings. It was then that he was first introduced to the space art of Scriven Bolton and Lucien Rudaux. After returning to the U.S., Bonestell returned to architectural designing and worked on such projects as the Supreme Court Building in Washington, D.C., the Chrysler Building in New York City, and San Francisco's Golden Gate Bridge. Using his specialized knowledge of perspective and the highly representational painting techniques architectural rendering required, he went to work in the late 1930s as a special-effects matte painter in Hollywood. His artwork can be seen in such films as *Citizen Kane, Only Angels Have Wings, The Magnificent Ambersons, The Hunchback of Notre Dame,* and *How Green Was My Valley.*

In 1944, *Life* published a series of paintings showing the planet Saturn as seen from some of its satellites. These were the first printed astronomical paintings by Bonestell. He used his knowledge of camera angles, perspective, and a life-long interest in astronomy to produce the most plausibly realistic portrayals of other worlds yet done. This immediately led to a virtual full-time career in space art. He provided technical advice and special-effects artwork for the classic science-fiction films *War of the Worlds, Destination Moon,* and *The Conquest of Space.* He provided much of the art for the great *Collier's* series on space flight, which were later transformed into the classic books, *Conquest of the Moon, The Exploration of Mars,* and *Across the Space Frontier* (authored by Wernher von Braun, Fred Whipple, Willy Ley, and others). His earliest astronomical paintings were gathered into his first book, with text by Willy Ley, *The Conquest of Space,* a best-seller in 1949 and now a highly-prized collector's item.

He painted several murals, notably a 10' x 40' panorama of the lunar surface for the Boston Museum of Science, which is now in the National Air and Space Museum in Washington, D.C. He has had numerous one-man shows, including two at the Smithsonian Institution—a very rare distinction. He has received the Science Fiction Special Achievement Award, the British Interplanetary Society Special Award and Medallion for lifetime accomplishments in space exploration, and the Dorothea Kumke Roberts Award from the Astronomical Society of the Pacific.

Bonestell's career has not only documented the development of space exploration, but has, in very large and unique measure, contributed to its final success. The persuasive, photographic realism of his paintings, combined with a nineteenth-century romanticism and sense of wonder, helped to convince a skeptical nation of taxpayers that the exploration of space was not only a very beautiful dream, but that it was well within the grasp of reality. □

The surface of Mercury, from the classic book, The Conquest of Space, *1949. By Chesley Bonestell (Frederick C. Durant, III Collection, courtesy of the artist).*

This painting was done for the Collier's space series. It shows a fleet of von Braun-designed spacecraft in Earth orbit, just before leaving for Mars. The small spacecraft carry personnel, and the large-winged craft are intended for the descent to the Martian surface. Only the small ships will make the round trip. By Chesley Bonestell (Adams Collection, courtesy of the artist).

Right: *Saturn, as seen from its largest moon, Titan.*
Below: *Painted for the* Life *Magazine series, "The World We Live In": Earth's continents congeal, incessantly bombarded by meteorites. On the horizon looms a swollen moon (Starlog Collection).*
Bottom: *Painted for the cover of* Man and the Moon, *1961: the exploration of the Jura Mountains on the Sinus Iridum, as seen from a crater in Mare Imbrium. All by Chesley Bonestell (courtesy of the artist).*

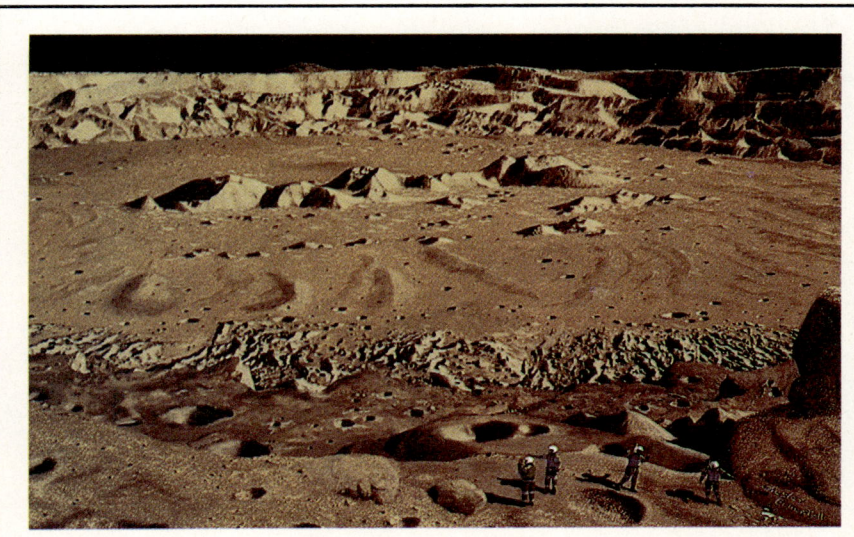

Top: *A team of astronauts explore the lunar crater Copernicus* (Ron Miller Collection).
Above: *A lunar landscape* (Smithsonian Institution Collection).
Left: *A ground station on Mars*, for The Exploration of Mars, 1956 (Smithsonian Institution Collection).
All by Chesley Bonestell (courtesy of the artist).

Overleaf: *Saturn, as it appears in the sky of its satellite, Iapetus. Although nine times further from Iapetus than our Moon is from Earth, giant Saturn still appears four times larger than a terrestrial full Moon.* First published in Life, 1944. By Chesley Bonestell (courtesy of the artist).

BOB McCALL

Bob McCall, born in 1919 in Columbus, Ohio, has had a life-long interest in art and aerospace subjects. As a child he liked to draw airplanes and armored knights and remembers: "I liked airplanes, because they made a lot of noise and were dramatic and moved fast—all the things kids like airplanes for. The knights in armor, now that I look back, are not unlike astronauts in space suits, and represent some of the same things to me: man adventurous, risking everything, facing new challenges. . . ."

McCall studied art on a scholarship at the Columbus College of Art and Design and the Art Institute of Chicago. During World War II, he was an Army Air Corps bombardier instructor, flying B-17s, B-21s, and B-24s. He has maintained close ties with the Air Force, travelling around the world to produce documentary art for the Air Force's art collection. After his military service, he worked as an illustrator with Bielefeld Studios in Chicago and then the Charles E. Cooper Studios in New York. In addition to his aviation and space work (and he currently specializes—although not exclusively, by any means—in the latter), he has worked in a wide range of advertising, industrial, and general editorial and story illustration in most of the major magazines. Like many of today's top illustrators, some of McCall's first work appeared in SF—one of his first was a cover for *Amazing Quarterly*.

McCall was naturally enthusiastic when the space program began in the 1950s. Contacting *Life* magazine, he began covering not only the infant space efforts, but future concepts as well. That work eventually led to his advertising art for the film, *2001: A Space Odyssey,* which was his springboard to fame within the genre of science fiction and speculative technical art. The originals of these posters are now in the collection of the National Air and Space Museum, where many of his other paintings are exhibited.

McCall produced artwork for a coffee-table volume, with text by Isaac Asimov, titled *Our World in Space,* which illustrated concepts of space exploration and colonization from the very near tomorrow to the very imaginative future. Since *2001,* McCall has been involved in conceptualizations for motion pictures, working very closely in the preproduction stages of science-fiction projects for Walt Disney, Doug Trumbull, and others.

McCall was among the first artists to be invited to take part in NASA's fine arts program and has continued to document the manned space program. One of his newest paintings to join the NASA collection depicts the rollout of the space shuttle *Enterprise.* He has also designed commemorative postage stamps, book jackets, and what must be one of the most-photographed works of art in the nation's capitol: a six-story-high mural for the National Air and Space Museum. ☐

Early settlement of the Moon will be work-horsed by functional, cylindrical spacecraft, as envisioned here by Bob McCall (courtesy of the artist).

An astronaut activates his (or her) portable rocket unit, creating a brilliant display of light in Earth orbit. Below are a space station and advanced shuttle vehicles. The majesty of this painting conveys the artist's spirit of wonder about outer space. By Bob McCall (courtesy of the artist).

Above: *Construction of a Gerard O'Neill-type space habitat around the year 2000, from a cover of* Future Magazine, *1978 (*Starlog *Collection).*
Right: *Vehicles are launched from a futuristic, anti-gravity city, as it hovers over the Grand Canyon. Both by Bob McCall (courtesy of the artist).*

Overleaf: *A spacecraft propelled by detonating atomic bombs in a spherical chamber. By Bob McCall (courtesy of the artist).*

LUDEK PESEK

Ludek Pesek (born 1919) first came to the attention of American readers with his spectacular debut in the August, 1970, *National Geographic* article,"Voyage to the Planets," for which he had provided fifteen color paintings. This was followed by "Journey to Mars" for the same magazine, which included a poster-size reproduction of a painting of a Martian dust storm. He has since appeared in several U.S. publications: *Smithsonian*, again in *National Geographic, Starlog,* and others.

Pesek's art is closer in manner of execution to Lucien Rudaux's than to Chesley Bonestell's. Rather than creating a pseudo-photograph, Pesek paints landscapes in a loose, almost impressionistic manner, which only suggests detail. However, his scenes are so natural-looking, without any appearance of invention or artificiality, that the viewer accepts them as representations of reality. He also possesses one of the most original imaginations of all the astronomical artists. While staying well within the limits of scientific accuracy, he is still able to create new and exciting ways to see subjects that may have been painted a dozen times by other artists.

A Czechoslovakian expatriate now living in Switzerland, Pesek had already attained a European reputation for his award-winning novels and photo-books before his first volume of astronomical paintings, *The Moon and the Planets,* was published. This over-size collection of forty double-page illustrations was translated in Italian, English, Japanese, and Russian, and received an honorable mention at the International Biennial of Illustration in 1966. It was followed by a companion volume in 1967, *Our Planet Earth,* which traced,in forty color paintings, the history of the Earth's surface from its creation to the present day. That year Pesek also wrote his first two science-fiction novels, *Log of a Moon Expedition* and *The Earth is Near.* The two over-size picture books first brought him to the attention of Frederick C. Durant, III, Assistant Director of the Smithsonian Institution's National Air and Space Museum, who in turn introduced Pesek to the *National Geographic.* Several of Pesek's paintings can be found in the permanent collection of the Smithsonian Institution, as well as in private collections.

In the half-dozen years following his *National Geographic* work, Pesek has illustrated and written many books: *UFOs, The Ocean World, Journey to the Planets, Planet Earth* (all with text by Peter Ryan and published by Penguin Books), *Space Shuttles* (with Bruno Stanek), *Flight to the World of Tomorrow,* and the magnificent *Bildatlas des Sonnensytems* (with text by Stanek). The latter coffee-table-size volume (whose title in English is *Picture Atlas of the Solar System*) contains thirty-eight color paintings, the bulk of them full or double-page reproductions.

Right, above: *Exploring a Martian "river channel."* Right, below: *The Martian south polar cap, covered with a mixture of carbon dioxide ("dry ice") and water.* Both by Ludek Pesek (courtesy of the artist).

A moonquake in the lunar highlands has shaken loose a pair of boulders that have rolled down a slope—an event recorded by Lunar Orbiter photographs. By Ludek Pesek (courtesy of the artist).